Original title:
Life, Laughter, and Unfinished Business

Copyright © 2025 Creative Arts Management OÜ
All rights reserved.

Author: Dorian Ashford
ISBN HARDBACK: 978-1-80566-271-6
ISBN PAPERBACK: 978-1-80566-566-3

The Kaleidoscope of Pending Chances

In swirling colors, dreams collide,
A dance of whims that never hide.
Each twist reveals a chuckled fate,
Where every sigh can still create.

Tick-tock goes the clock's old tune,
We juggle moments, make them swoon.
With every laugh, a chance to bend,
In the kaleidoscope, there's no end.

A Mirthful Glimpse Through Time

Snapshots lost in glee's embrace,
Memories chase at a breathless pace.
We trip on echoes from the past,
In time's embrace, we hope to last.

Winks and giggles, tales unfold,
With each new laugh, we're never old.
The clock may tick, yet here we stand,
In laughter's grip, just hand in hand.

The Heartbeat of Forgotten Commitments

Promises float like bubbles bright,
Popped by chuckles in the night.
We dance around what we once swore,
Yet still we crave for just one more.

With every giggle, plans may fade,
But tasks undone keep the fun made.
In every heartbeat, joy persists,
While laughter lingers, we coexist.

Unfinished Mischief in the Air

Whispers of pranks still take their flight,
  Hovering softly, slipped from sight.
  Every chuckle hints at a scheme,
In half-formed tricks, we still can dream.

  Doodles of plans scribble the night,
  Every mischief feels just right.
  In corners where shadows play,
  We sip our tea, laugh, and sway.

Beckoning Moments Await

In a world of quirky chance,
Where silly dreams refuse to dance.
Ticklish breezes swirl and twirl,
As laughter bubbles, joy unfurl.

Beneath the sun's bright, playful rays,
We chase our whims in silly ways.
A stumble here, a giggle there,
In every moment, magic's flair.

A Symphony of Unfinished Stories

In the hallway, echoes play,
With socks that wander far away.
A tale begins but never ends,
As time turns tricks, our joy ascends.

Forgotten notes and laughter's tune,
A dance beneath the silver moon.
Each story pauses, then resumes,
In shadows cast by bright balloons.

Footsteps on Dusty Trails

With every step, the ground will sigh,
As mysteries weave and laughter flies.
A slip on leaves, a shout, a cheer,
We wander freely, never fear.

The road is long, the path unclear,
But friends beside us, always near.
In the dust, we find our gold,
With jokes and tales forever told.

Unanswered Echoes in Empty Rooms

In corners where the giggles hide,
With echoes that refuse to bide.
A wink, a nod, a fleeting glance,
As memories swirl in playful dance.

The walls remember joy's embrace,
Where antics leave a light trace.
Though silence lingers, we shall see,
The laughter lives in you and me.

The Memory of a Laugh

In the corner, a joke still spins,
Like a pinwheel caught in the wind.
We giggle at shadows that dance and sway,
Chasing worries that fade away.

A chicken crossed, or so they claim,
To reach the other side, just the same.
Frogs in tuxedos tap dance in line,
As I fumble for pennies to buy some time.

Under the table, lost socks reside,
Whispers of laughter, a cozy inside.
The cat takes a leap, a slow-motion fall,
A slapstick routine that entertains all.

With ice cream cones and sprinkles of cheer,
We build our castles, our fortifications here.
Each chuckle like bricks, sturdy and bright,
Creating a fortress that glimmers with light.

Stars that Wait for Dawn

The moon tells secrets to squirrels in trees,
While crickets host shows that hum with ease.
Balloons of laughter float high in the air,
As dreams twist and twirl without a care.

Twinkling stars share their glittery tales,
Of comets and space, of the wind in their sails.
A cosmic circus, the cosmos in bloom,
Where punchlines erupt from a nebula's room.

We sip from our mugs, full of jokes and glee,
The sunlight whispers, "Just wait and see!"
Tomorrow will come, but tonight we play,
With echoes of giggles that dance and sway.

So grab a good pun and hold it tight,
As the world spins madly into the night.
For every good chuckle, a spark of delight,
In this grand tapestry woven so bright.

Unopened Letters Underneath the Bed

Dusty stacks with secrets kept,
Never read, just lightly wept.
Each line a giggle, a sigh, a jest,
A silent tale of a life unblessed.

Lost socks and dreams lie side by side,
Waiting for nods, a wry smile, a glide.
Postcards stacked, all from the past,
Memories fading, but laughter will last.

Tickled by words that haven't been said,
In the chaos, joy overhead.
Crumbs of humor, crumbs of cheer,
In unopened letters, it's all right here.

Melancholy in the Giddy Hour

Twilight dances on the edge of jest,
With each chuckle, the heart's a quest.
A fumbled drink, a sassy toast,
In the playful moments, we cherish the most.

Smiles wrapped in the shadows of light,
Where sullen thoughts take flight.
A giggle slips through a tearful glance,
In this crazy, cluttered dance.

Moments drift with whirls of cheer,
In the giddy hour, madness draws near.
Between the giggles and the sighs,
Melancholy sometimes wears disguise.

The Weight of Uncollected Moments

Heavy hearts and lighter dreams,
Collecting laughter like rippling streams.
Each tick of time, a whispered pun,
While silly thoughts race, oh what fun!

Balloons of wishes fill the air,
With unturned corners, we seldom dare.
Hold tight those fragments of the day,
For in their laughter, we'll find our way.

Jokes left hanging, the punchline missed,
In a maze of chuckles, we coexist.
Weightless giggles, moments amassed,
In the ledger of joy, none are cast.

Treasures Yet to Be Found

X marks the spot where memories hide,
In the attic of laughter, we glide.
Pieces of joy all wrapped in gold,
Tales of mischief waiting to be told.

Buried treasures in plain sight,
Amidst the chaos, pure delight.
Lost in the shuffle of daily grind,
Sweet little gems left behind.

Adventures missed, but still we roam,
In the garden of giggles, we build our home.
Chasing shadows of moments unspooled,
In this playful life, we're always fooled.

The Promise of Tomorrow's Light

In the glow of a morning grin,
We chase shadows and giggles within.
Plans scribbled in haste on a napkin,
Tomorrow's whims, where fun begins.

With each tick of the clock, we play,
Pretending the dishes just melt away.
Socks mismatched and stories absurd,
We'll dance in the chaos, undeterred.

Secret Smiles in Passing Time

A wink shared in the grocery line,
Produce throwing its best punchline.
The cat next door, in a top hat perched,
Whispers secrets that leave us lurching.

In the park, we trade silly jokes,
Falling off benches, we're just folks.
The clouds chuckle, they know the score,
That laughter loops and opens doors.

Paths Not Taken

Maps forgotten in the drawer's tight hold,
Picturing roads with stories untold.
We stroll where the sidewalk cracks and skips,
With a smirk for each bump in our trips.

Lost in a maze of half-baked dreams,
Navigating chaos and silly schemes.
Behind every corner, a giggle does dwell,
We'll toast to the mishaps; they ring like a bell.

Tides of Unwritten Wishes

With a flip of the coin, we cast our fate,
Sailing on a sea where the fish all skate.
Each wave carries secrets, each splash a grin,
Wishing wells filled with chuckles within.

Stranded on shores of forgotten delight,
Where jellybeans grow under the moonlight.
We catch joy as it tumbles and rolls,
A treasure of laughter, nourishing souls.

The Giggle of a Half-Remembered Joke

A chuckle slips from a distance,
Half-formed thoughts dance in the air.
We chase the laughter's insistence,
But memories play a mischievous dare.

In corners of minds they gather,
Whispers of punchlines yet to be.
Each twist and turn feeds the lather,
As riddles bloom, wild and free.

They echo like a tune forgotten,
With every slip, we find the glee.
Our thoughts entwined, though often rotten,
In hilarity, we choose to be.

So here's to giggles in moments lost,
We'll keep them close—whatever the cost.

Open Chapters in a Closed Book

Pages turned but not forgotten,
Whispers linger in the lines.
Tales of dragons, dreams begotten,
In margins, inked with playful signs.

The plot thickens like a soup,
Characters waltz through forgotten schemes.
Close your eyes and take a swoop,
Reality fades—welcome dreams.

Words may scatter, but we hold tight,
To tales that twist and time forgets.
A dance of humor, out of sight,
In open chapters, no regrets.

So let us read beyond the spine,
In laughter's glow, the world aligns.

The Unraveled Thread of Existence

Oh, tangled yarn, where do you lead?
Knit and purl of days that weave.
A stitch or two, a madman's creed,
In knots of joy, we laugh, believe.

Each fray holds tales of chaos spun,
Like socks with holes, we wear our pride.
With every fumble, there's some fun,
In the mess, our joys abide.

Threads of mishaps spill on the floor,
Every loose end a wink in disguise.
We dance around, forever unsure,
Yet find delight under open skies.

So pull that string, let laughter ring,
In the tapestry of everything.

Hearts Left Unspoken

In silent rooms where echoes play,
Words hover like butterflies.
Unsaid feelings often sway,
Caught in the web of secret sighs.

A grin exchanged, a wink too sly,
Hopeful glances, mischief ignites.
Hearts weave stories as time slips by,
In the quiet, we share our flights.

Chasing shadows of affection,
Through laughter, our fears lie low.
In this dance of mild rejection,
We find a fun in what we owe.

So here's to whispers, soft and light,
In spaces where thoughts take flight.

The Sweet Serenade of Now and Then

In the garden of lost time, we breeze,
Where giggles dance on honeyed leaves.
We chase echoes of yesterday's cheer,
With painted faces, we conquer fear.

Chasing shadows on an endless race,
We toss our worries, make room for grace.
Each moment a wink, a jest we share,
In the tapestry of now, we declare.

From balloons that float to jokes that glide,
Every tick of the clock is a joyful ride.
With candy dreams and whims that sprout,
In the serenade of now, we sing out loud.

A melody sweet, with notes of delight,
We weave our laughter into the night.
In the embrace of moments so rare,
We'll spin tales of wonder, everywhere.

A Cup Overflowing with Hope's Brew

In a cup brimming full, we sip and smile,
Flavor of dreams adds sweetness to the trial.
With sprinkles of joy to lighten the load,
Each sip brings a chuckle, on the road.

Stirring the pot of bright surprises,
Laughter bubbles like joyful disguises.
With every slurp, the world seems clear,
An elixir of whimsy, always near.

In the warmth of the brew, we find our cheer,
Every drop a promise that beckons us near.
With mugs raised high, we toast the unknown,
Each gulp a reminder we're never alone.

So let us savor this cup of delight,
With a pinch of madness to make it just right.
As long as the kettle sings its sweet tune,
We'll dance through the shadows beneath the moon.

The Symphony of All That's Left to Be

In the concert of dreams, we play our part,
Missed notes and stumbles are just the start.
With a tap of the shoe and a wink of the eye,
We'll compose a jest as time slips by.

Each chord we strike has a twist and a turn,
As the sound of the silly begins to churn.
With laughter as a metronome to our beat,
We sway through the chaos, light on our feet.

Harmonies wander through canyons of awe,
Resonating with giggles that never withdraw.
In the grand hall of what lies still ahead,
Every unfinished line is a dance instead.

As the curtain descends, we bow with glee,
For every note played is our legacy.
With unfinished tunes in a delightful fray,
We'll keep on composing, come what may.

Gentle Reminders from the Golden Past

In the attic of whispers, we rummage with flair,
Dusty boxes hide chuckles beyond compare.
With pictures that grin and stories anew,
We sip from the fountain of moments we threw.

Faded laughter wraps us in warm coats,
Every tale a treasure, like whimsical notes.
With echoes of giggles ringing so clear,
In the scrapbook of memories, we find our cheer.

Tickled by time, the clock plays its tricks,
As we juggle our dreams, dodging the picks.
With playful nudges from the days gone by,
We brandish our quirks like stars in the sky.

So gather your smiles, embrace the delight,
In the dances of yesteryear, we'll take flight.
For in every soft whisper of times we miss,
Lie gentle reminders of laughter's sweet bliss.

Dreams Adrift on the Breeze

Wishing wells with coins that sing,
Float along like paper things.
Kites that dance on sunny days,
Chasing clouds in whimsical ways.

Socks that vanish, where do they go?
Riddles hidden in the snow.
Sunsets play in colors bold,
Stories waiting to be told.

Jumping jacks on twilight grass,
Counting stars as dreams amass.
Cupcakes frosted, smiles arise,
Laughter echoes in the skies.

Whimsical winds will blow us high,
With every giggle, we can fly.
Adventures call with open arms,
Embracing all their silly charms.

Serendipity in the Unplanned

Socks mismatched, what a sight,
Coffee spills at morning light.
Fumbling keys in pockets deep,
Twirling tales we like to keep.

Umbrellas flipping in the storm,
Making chaos feel so warm.
Forgotten lunches left behind,
Finding treasures, oh so blind.

Plans that stumble, joy takes flight,
Unexpected sparks ignite.
Wandering paths we didn't seek,
Discoveries make our hearts speak.

Giggles shared with strangers near,
Magic moments always cheer.
In the mess, we find the gold,
Stories waiting to unfold.

The Echo of a Faded Laugh

Chasing echoes down the hall,
Ticklish whispers, can't stand tall.
Pillows fight in sleep's embrace,
Memory games we all can trace.

Old jokes linger in the air,
Nostalgic smiles, joy to share.
Funny faces in the glass,
Laughter lingers, never past.

Pictures taken, silly grins,
Moments captured, where it begins.
Jumping on beds, what a spree,
With every giggle, we feel free.

Time may fade those sounds we know,
Yet in hearts, they always glow.
Playful spirits never fade,
Treasured giggles softly laid.

Adventures Beyond the Horizon

Maps are scribbles, paths unclear,
With every step, we conquer fear.
In cardboard boxes, dreams take flight,
Exploring realms of day and night.

Pirates sailing on a whim,
With make-believe, our sails brim.
Combatting shadows, fears abound,
Yet in joy, true treasures found.

Every stumble, a dance of glee,
With hugs and laughter, wild and free.
Whirlwinds swirling around our feet,
In the chaos, we find the beat.

So let's embark, no end in sight,
Journey onward, hearts so light.
With every twist, the fun begins,
Crafting tales through silly spins.

Dancing Shadows on a Sunlit Path

In the garden, gnomes do prance,
While daisies sway, they take a chance.
Laughter lingers in the breeze,
As squirrels plot their nutty tease.

Sunbeams waltz on cobblestone,
Chasing giggles, never alone.
Bubbles burst in joyful flight,
Turning frowns to pure delight.

The wind plays tricks on the trees,
Tickling branches, making them sneeze.
Butterflies flirt, they swirl and twirl,
As the world spins in a vibrant whirl.

And shadows dance, side by side,
With ancient tunes in playful pride.
A whimsical tune floats through the air,
A sweet reminder to laugh and share.

Echoes of Joy in the Quiet Air

In a cozy nook, the kettle sings,
While the cat dreams of fanciful things.
Laughter spills like tasty tea,
As cookies crumble, wild and free.

A tickle in the vibrant night,
Stars crack jokes with twinkling light.
The moon grins with a knowing glance,
As shadows gather to join the dance.

Echoes glide on winds that swirl,
Whispering secrets in a twirl.
A snail joins in the fun parade,
Wearing a hat that grandma made.

In quiet corners, giggles bloom,
Chasing away the glum and gloom.
A symphony of chuckles play,
Reminding all to seize the day.

Whispers of Tomorrow's Dreams

Sunrise paints the sky with cheer,
As toast pops up with a quirky sneer.
Jams and jellies compete for fame,
While pancakes flip with a silly name.

Socks mismatched, a fashion spree,
As children giggle on the spree.
Invisible friends join the fun,
In a world that's just begun.

A kite takes off, so bold and bright,
With wishes tied, it takes to flight.
The breeze whispers tales anew,
Of dreams fulfilled and journeys due.

In this dance of time and chance,
Each moment offers a giggling glance.
So we chase tomorrow's glowing beam,
With smiles wide, we dare to dream.

Chasing Clouds of Forgotten Smiles

In the attic, boxes wait,
Filled with treasures, small and great.
Old photographs of silly grins,
Remind us where the fun begins.

A stampede of socks on the floor,
Each with a story, maybe more.
While crayons wheel, drawing the day,
Our imaginations run away.

The clock ticks slow, yet time flies fast,
As giggles echo from the past.
Clouds of mischief float above,
With playful nudges and gentle love.

So let's dive deep, embrace the jest,
In the joy of moments, we are blessed.
Chasing whispers, we find our way,
And gather smiles like bright bouquet.

The Canvas of Tomorrow

Each morning brings a chance to play,
With colors bright, we dance and sway.
A splash of blue, a stroke of red,
We paint our dreams where visions spread.

The sun peeks in, a cheeky grin,
As we create, let chaos win.
With every brush, a joke takes flight,
In this mural of delight so bright.

Who needs a map to guide the way?
When giggles lead, it's sure to sway.
We mix our hues in clumsy glee,
And laugh out loud at what will be.

Though edges blur and outlines fade,
The picture's charm will not evade.
For in this art, we find our glow,
A canvas bright for all to know.

Paintbrushes Still Wet

With paint-stained hands, we make our mark,
In swirling colors, we simply spark.
Each stroke a story, silly and bold,
In drips and drops, our fate unfolds.

Like toddlers painting on the walls,
We giggle loud as laughter calls.
A whimsy here, a splash and dash,
A masterpiece from moments flash.

We duck and dodge the looming fate,
Creating joy while we await.
With sticky fingers, we craft our dreams,
In vibrant shades, it's all as it seems.

Though the clocks tick on with quiet pace,
We savor each moment in this space.
Our brushes dance, the colors blend,
A joyful mess that won't soon end.

The Sound of Unwritten Pages

Empty sheets whisper tales untold,
With every blank, new worlds unfold.
A humorous bird, flutters in flight,
Chasing the ink with pure delight.

Quills dance wildly, a chaotic rhyme,
We scribble nonsense, it's party time!
With every giggle, the plot gets thick,
And laughter spills — oh, what a trick!

Each page a stage for whimsy's show,
Where silly thoughts are free to grow.
We dash through lines, no room for fear,
As laughter lingers, ever near.

The pen may pause, but hearts don't quit,
In this tale of jest, we fully commit.
For every story begins with play,
As humor shines through every display.

Laughter Between the Cracks

In sidewalks worn and streets so cracked,
We find the grins that laughter tracked.
Beneath the bench, a squirrel does dance,
While strangers pause, lost in a glance.

A giggle escapes from clouds above,
As rainbows pop like bursts of love.
With every fumble, we cheer and shout,
In every blunder, there's joy throughout.

The world is silly, just take a peek,
At wobbly steps and the joy we seek.
We gather moments like treasures bright,
In the cracks of day, admiration's light.

So join the fun, come let's collide,
With a wink, we dance in fate's sly glide.
For in the laughter, we claim our space,
In chaos sweet, we find our grace.

The Dance of Daydreams and Detours

In a tutu made of wishes, they twirl,
Chasing shadows in a bustling swirl.
With every step, the mishaps bloom,
Creating laughter in the crowded room.

A misstep here, oh what a sight,
Spinning stories in the dimming light.
Each pratfall echoes like a cheer,
As we maneuver through the atmosphere.

With each turn, we twist fate's knuckle,
Stepping lightly through the joyful muckle.
Unplanned routes lead to the best delight,
Painting the chaos in colors bright.

In the twilight, the giggles burst,
As we dance in rhythm, and wanderlust.
With every twirl, new tales to share,
Unraveled dreams hang thick in the air.

Unseen Journeys and Stalled Adventures

In a cardboard box or a paper boat,
We sail through tales that never wrote.
The compass spins, oh where to go?
Destination lost in the afterglow.

Maps of giggles and paths of sighs,
Adventures linger where humor lies.
The bus is late, but who cares the most?
We gather crumbs and make a toast.

Each detour brings a clownish mime,
Creating stories, one step at a time.
With coffee spills and misplaced socks,
We accumulate laughs like ticking clocks.

The journey pauses, yet we remain,
Finding joy in the mundane rain.
Every wrong turn becomes a prize,
With silly repartees that mesmerize.

Tides of Laughter Against the Shore of Time

Waves cresting high, spinning in glee,
Silly moments, as bright as can be.
Surfboards made of dreams and jest,
Riding the currents, we feel so blessed.

Every splash tells a tale anew,
With seaweed crowns and fishes' view.
We dance with dolphins, a playful crew,
As time drifts by in a watery blue.

The sandcastles crumble, but we don't frown,
As nature's laughter splashes us down.
Sunsets painted with hearty grins,
With every tide, the fun begins.

With echoes of joy in the evening breeze,
We gather our treasures, just as we please.
Footprints in jest, washed away in rhyme,
In the waves of the moment, we conquer time.

Palette of Colors Yet to Be Mixed

Splashes of yellow with a dash of blue,
A canvas dreams of a wacky crew.
Each brushstroke tells a tale of cheer,
With vibrant hues, we shed every fear.

A swirl of red wrapped in green,
A masterpiece of mischief unseen.
With every layer, the humor grows,
Like a garden blooming with quirky prose.

Spilling paint like laughter bright,
Crafting stories until the night.
Every hue dances, every shade sings,
Creating joy in the simplest things.

In the palette, the colors blend,
A tapestry of fun that we defend.
With unfinished strokes, we plot and plan,
Turning the mundane into a joyful jam.

A Journey Tethered to Unsaid Words

On a road where whispers play,
Unraveled tales from yesterday.
We dance with dreams and stuttered sighs,
A chuckle hidden beneath the skies.

Left behind are socks and thoughts,
In the midst of tangled knots.
We chase the bus that never shows,
And laugh at all our silly woes.

Forgotten cakes left on the shelf,
We toast to ghosts and to ourselves.
A merry chase, a jest untold,
With every stumble, our hearts unfold.

As dawn peeks out, tickled and bright,
We leap for joy, a comical flight.
For in the wings, our tales await,
And jesters roam through every gate.

Harvesting Joy from the Fields of Time

In gardens green where giggles grow,
We pick the fruits of joy to sow.
With every weed, a laugh we find,
As sunlight paints the petals blind.

The scarecrow's grin, a lopsided charm,
In the dance of bees, there's naught to harm.
We trip on roots, we glide on air,
As laughter ripples, banishing care.

Clouds above like cotton candy fluff,
The breeze whispers tales, sweet and tough.
Embracing moments, wild and free,
We spin in circles, giddy with glee.

Oh, the harvest is a funny game,
Each stumble, a badge we gladly claim.
For in this field, with dreams entwined,
We're jesters, my friend, forever inclined.

Moments Yet to Be

The clock spins tales, a jester's song,
In moments where we all belong.
With every tick, a chance to jest,
In this circus, we are the best.

Clouds parade with fluffy hats,
While raindrops dance like playful cats.
Each instant winks, a teasing glance,
Inviting all to join the dance.

Forgotten snacks lost in the fray,
Bring giggles loud, in a quirky way.
With every stumble, with every fall,
We ride the wave, we hear the call.

So let the moments weave and play,
In this grand circus of every day.
For what's to come is yet unclear,
But oh, the fun is always near!

Echoes of Unsaid Words

In quiet halls where echoes dwell,
Whispers bounce, casting a spell.
The twinkle of eyes, the mischief's glow,
Hiding truths we never know.

A wink shared, a sly remark,
Turns ordinary into a spark.
As laughter lingers in the air,
We gather moments, a jovial fare.

The fridge hums tunes of meals undone,
Where stale bread waits for a bit of fun.
With every bite, a chuckle blooms,
In the chaos of our crowded rooms.

So let us drink to all that's said,
And to the words that dance in our head.
For in the echoes, we find our tune,
And weave our stories beneath the moon.

The Beauty of Approaching Storms

Clouds gather, a jester in gray,
Thunder chuckles, lighting the way.
Raindrops tap dance on rooftops, they prance,
Nature's symphony is a wild romance.

Hats fly off; umbrellas take flight,
Dancing in puddles, a jubilant sight.
Lightning cracks jokes in the darkening sky,
As we shiver and giggle, oh me, oh my.

A rainbow sneaks in, painting the gloom,
Tickling the air with its vibrant plume.
Kites laugh as they soar in gusty winds,
Every droplet a whisper, joy never ends.

Storms may threaten, but we'll carry on,
With belly laughs echoing 'til the dawn.
A cosmic comedy, the world in jest,
Finding fun in chaos, we are truly blessed.

What Lies Beyond the Threshold

A door creaks open to whimsical cheer,
Curiosity beckoning, drawing you near.
Each step is a giggle, a playful tease,
Exploring the unknown, amongst the trees.

An attic of wonders and long-lost toys,
Echoes of laughter from soft little joys.
In shadows we chase the glimmers of light,
Unfolding the secrets hidden from sight.

The porch swing whispers tales of old,
Each creak a story waiting to be told.
Mismatched chairs, they inspire a jest,
Invite you to sit, forget all the rest.

Outside the realm of predictability,
We twirl and we leap, oh, so carefree!
Every twist and turn, a mystery spun,
Step into the playful, let the fun run.

Imprints of a Wandering Mind

Thoughts float like bubbles, popping in glee,
Drifting through clouds, as light as can be.
Ideas swirl round, a carnival ride,
With laughter that giggles and won't be denied.

Sketching grand castles in the sand, so bright,
Cloudy creatures dance in the soft twilight.
Chasing daydreams, we run wild and free,
Turning mundane moments into a spree.

A roaming spirit, with pockets of wit,
Every quirky notion just begs to commit.
Words tumble and tumble, like leaves in the breeze,
Giving life to mischief, as they aim to please.

In the labyrinth of thoughts, there's joy to be found,
Each twist and each turn brings a chuckle profound.
Hold onto these whims, let them fly high,
For in the chase of mirth, we forever rely.

Conversations with the Wind

The breeze has a gossip, a tale to share,
Whispering secrets, tickling the air.
Rustling leaves join in with a giggling sound,
While paper planes soar, freedom unbound.

"Do you hear that?" asks the old oak tree,
"I'm the guardian of jest, can't you see?"
The wind laughs back, a playful delight,
Spinning around, making shadows take flight.

Clouds loom closer, with mischief in tow,
While shadows behind them make faces that glow.
From dried dandelions to grasses that sway,
The chatter of nature brightens the day.

So dance with the whispers, let laughter be sent,
For joy rolls on quietly, never to relent.
In the keen caress of a breezy exchange,
Find the humor, let ordinary feel strange.

Sketches on the Back of Dreams

On napkins, visions dance away,
With crayons of forgotten play.
They giggle in the corners bright,
A masterpiece in morning light.

A sock without its perfect pair,
Sings songs that float upon the air.
Half-finished tales of yesteryear,
Emerge from jars, and bring a cheer.

The clock forgets to mark our time,
As doodles turn to words that rhyme.
An artist with no grand display,
Leaves laughter on the canvas gray.

With every scribble, joy expands,
We sketch our lives with messy hands.
In every line, a story's tossed,
Each chuckle hides a dream embossed.

Golden Threads of Pending Joy

A button lost upon the floor,
Tells secrets that we can't ignore.
It hops and skips with every glance,
Awaits the day for one more chance.

A cat with plans to rule the chairs,
Plotting schemes in sunshine's flares.
With every pounce, a giggle's born,
As yarns tangle, fates are worn.

Stickers on the fridge proclaim,
Mishaps turn to joyful game.
Between the old ketchup and spice,
Lives a quest for fun, so nice.

And in the shadows, dreams take flight,
With humor twinkling through the night.
Each step we take, a dance of glee,
For every joy that's yet to be.

The Dance of the Undone

A towel now a superhero,
Swings wildly on the bathroom floor.
Half-sewn socks, a costume bright,
Sparkle in the morning light.

With mismatched shoes, we strut our way,
Each step a note in life's ballet.
We twirl in circles, skip, and spin,
Chasing dreams that can't begin.

The popcorn bowl's an island lost,
On seas of fluff, we count the cost.
Laughter echoes from the past,
Dodging chores that never last.

And so we sway to music strange,
Embracing all that feels so deranged.
Each unfinished tune will find its beat,
In every breath, in every heartbeat.

Flickers of Past Joys

A photo fades but not the giggle,
Memories play and do a little wiggle.
In every frame, a tale unfolds,
Of silly dances and dreams retold.

The cake that fell, a sweet surprise,
As frosting dripped and laughter flies.
With every fail, a victory grows,
In crumbs of joy, our spirit flows.

The kite that crashed upon the tree,
Still whispers winds of fun and glee.
Unfinished poems on the shelf,
Whisper secrets of our true self.

So here we gather, tales in hand,
In fragments of a vivid land.
These flickers of our yesterdays,
Shall light the path in funny ways.

The Puzzle of What Might Have Been

Jigsaw pieces scattered wide,
Memories tangled, they'll abide.
Each corner's close, yet still askew,
What could have been, but never grew.

A missing chunk beneath the bed,
It holds the dreams that danced and fled.
With chuckles shared, and sighs between,
This puzzler's wild, and yet it's keen.

In crowded rooms, the echoes ring,
Of chances lost, but oh, the zing!
We laugh aloud, though it feels strange,
What luck it seems, in all this change.

So raise a toast, to all the mess,
Embrace the chaos, nothing less.
For in the end, the smiles we glean,
Outshine the gaps where dreams have been.

Twists of Fortune in a Comic Script

In scripts unwritten, plots collide,
With awkward slips and quirky pride.
The hero stumbles, trips on fate,
A comic gem, don't make us wait!

A twist of fate, a missing cue,
The villain flops, the crowd cries 'boo!'
Yet laughter bubbles, fills the air,
These hilarious bloopers, oh so rare.

Chasing shadows in broad daylight,
We find the punchline, what a sight!
With every flap, a new delight,
We dance through jokes; they take to flight.

So roll the dice, no need for care,
In this madplay, none are aware.
The plots may thicken, sure and bleak,
But laughter's our best, cheeky technique.

Threads of Muse in A Tattered Tale

Once upon a time, oh my,
A thread unspooled, no reason why.
In tangled yarn, odd colors blend,
A tapestry that seems to bend.

Characters sketched with wobbly hands,
In whimsical worlds, absurd demands.
The penguin dances, the cat can sing,
In this odd tale, what joy they bring!

Through twists and turns, we weave and stitch,
Each tangled line, a splendid glitch.
The end's unwritten, yet here we stand,
A joyful mess, a merry band.

So spin the yarn, let laughter flow,
In every thread, a chance to glow.
For life's a tale in wild disguise,
A tapestry spun from joyful highs.

A Glimpse Through Laughter's Veil

Behind the curtain, curtains rise,
A peek reveals a grand surprise.
In shadows dance, the jokes emerge,
A playful spirit, laughter's surge.

The rodent prince loses his shoe,
While out-of-tune birds sing askew.
With every flub, the crowd erupts,
Their giggles soar, as fate disrupts.

A jester bumbles, tipsy cheer,
Yet glimmers shine, when love is near.
Even mistakes become a game,
When humor's spark ignites the flame.

So take this bow, take on the night,
With gleeful gaffes, our hearts take flight.
Through laughter's veil, we boldly tread,
A dance of dreams, our fears misled.

The Unwritten Pages of My Story

In a world of quirky dreams,
I scribble hopes on napkin seams.
Each page holds a tale so bright,
Yet coffee spills steal the spotlight.

My sandwich talks, it's quite absurd,
It whispers secrets, not a word.
I chase the crumbs of joy, I swear,
While birds just giggle in midair.

To-do lists dance in mismatched shoes,
With every task, a playful ruse.
I laugh at time, it's just a jest,
An unpublished script, I'm not distressed.

So here's to moments yet to be,
With jumbled thoughts like a bumblebee.
I'll raise a toast, though half-baked too,
For every giggle that's overdue.

Serenade of Sighs and Sunshine

Beneath the beams, a snail does prance,
In messy hats, they take a chance.
A flower sneezes, what a scene,
As grinning daisies paint the green.

The socks in drawers conspire each night,
To stage a dance in moon's soft light.
And giggles bubble like a brook,
In every nook, delightful hook.

A teacup winks, it's got a tale,
Of sugar lumps and turkey's veil.
Let's spin the yarn of silly thoughts,
Where laughter ebbs and often rots.

So here's the tune, let's hum along,
With every chuckle, we can't go wrong.
The stage is set, come play a part,
In this quirky ballet of the heart.

Fragments of Laughter in the Breeze

A jester's cap atop a tree,
Giggling leaves blow wild and free.
The sunbeams tickle, skies paint smiles,
On wobbly chairs, we've got the styles.

The cookies bake, they dance and twirl,
While flour flies in a happy whirl.
But when they burn, oh what a jest,
A crunchy tale, but still the best.

Old photos wave, in faded cheer,
Of frizzy hair and fun-filled years.
With every snapshot, tales unfold,
In foolish frames, our hearts are sold.

Oh let's embrace the folly, dear,
For every giggle, there's no fear.
A patchwork quilt of silly days,
Where humor leads in quirky ways.

Unraveled Threads of Yesterday

In messy rooms, the yarn's awry,
As we chase dreams beneath the sky.
Each tangled laugh, a memory bright,
With sock puppets, we take flight.

The cat wears glasses, with such flair,
Pretending wisdom, it doesn't care.
The goldfish giggles, bubbles pop,
A wacky show, the heart won't stop.

The clock is late, it plays the fool,
Sipping sunshine in a kiddie pool.
With every tick, a chance to jest,
In jumbled hours, we find our best.

So let's embrace the wobbly ride,
With mismatched shoes, let's dance with pride.
For in this chaos, joy can bloom,
A splendid mess within the room.

The Road Not Fully Travelled

A path I took, but turned around,
With every step, a lost sound.
My shoes are worn, my socks mismatched,
On this route, I've hardly hatched.

I met a squirrel, it laughed at me,
A GPS set to 'wild and free'.
With charts and maps all tossed aside,
I grasped the fun, not where to glide.

Each turn's a joke, a playful tease,
Like socks that slip, I bend my knees.
The destination? I'll make it up!
For the journey's worth, I'll fill my cup.

So let's walk on, make merry and jest,
For wanderers know, it's not a test.
With every mishap, a story we weave,
In this joy ride, we laugh, believe.

Blossoms that Never Bloomed

In a garden where hopes did tease,
Petals unformed dance in the breeze.
Not every seed finds loyalty,
Some turn to jokes of futility.

A sunflower's pout on a rainy day,
"Why grow up?" it seems to say.
With weeds as friends, they jest and jest,
A bud that might, but won't contest.

The daisies snicker, the roses sigh,
In this patch, the dreams can fly.
No bloom to show, yet joy is rife,
In this hugging ground of awkward life.

So here's to blooms that chose to tease,
Their laughter echoes through the trees.
With giggles tucked in each green shoot,
They linger, never needing loot.

Unfinished Conversations at Midnight

The clock strikes twelve, with words unfurled,
In soft whispers, our thoughts swirled.
Yet pauses linger, like a pun gone stale,
We laugh too loud, our faces pale.

The toaster chimes, it joins the fight,
As we recall the silliest sight.
Each half-sentence takes on a life,
While shadows giggle, avoiding strife.

Over coffee cups, we plot and scheme,
In every silence, a wild dream.
Wander through thoughts, both deep and wide,
As conversations join this merry ride.

Though names may slip, and tales forget,
We find the joy in every jest.
Midnight's chance, to play and sway,
With unfinished lines, we laugh away.

When Time Plays Hide and Seek

Time's a prankster, pushing us 'round,
In hide and seek, it's never found.
We chase its tail, a fleeting breeze,
With giggles lost among the trees.

A watch that laughs with ticking grace,
As minutes sprint, they leave no trace.
The calendar winks with a silly grin,
"Catch me if you can," it says with sin.

Dinner's burnt, the cake a flop,
Yet every oops is a reason to hop.
With every 'oops' and every fall,
We rise again, we heed the call.

On this game board of sun and shade,
We find the fun that never fades.
So here's to time, our merry thief,
In laughter, we find our sweet relief.

The Question in Uncurled Leaves

In the park a squirrel doth dance,
With acorns hidden, caught in a trance.
A question hangs in the sunlit skies,
Why do birds sing? Oh, to summarize!

Beneath the tree, the shadows play,
A cat with dreams of catching prey.
But what of those who just lie still?
Are they plotting mischief or just chill?

The wind whispers tales of what was missed,
As paper boats sail, waved by the bliss.
Uncurled they wander, as gaps do show,
Is there more to know? Oh, where did they go?

While time rolls on, we laugh and shout,
Among the leaves, we'll twist about.
With each taunting breeze, the earth responds,
In ungrasped wishes, hilarity bonds.

Echoes of the Almost

A jester juggles dreams of delight,
While shadows stretch, fading from sight.
Echoes of laughter ring through the night,
Almost grasped, but taking flight.

In crooked chairs, we share our chat,
Of tangled tales and the odd fat cat.
The mishaps blend, a beautiful find,
The best kind of stories are often unlined.

As twilight giggles, the stars align,
With each tiny twinkle, there's always a sign.
Almost enough, yet barely the key,
We chase the spark in what might be.

So raise a toast to the maybes in life,
To the almost friends and the almost strife.
With smiles wrapped in a cozy spark,
Let's treasure the echoes that strike their mark.

A Tapestry of Anticipated Journeys

In crumpled tickets and maps unfurled,
Dreamers gather, a motley world.
With caffeine lines and cupcakes galore,
We sketch our travels, imagine and roar.

The bus left early, but where's my shoe?
As we board the train, I lose my cue.
Adventures await but plans are awry,
Laughter erupts, oh my, oh my!

Every stop whispered, a giggle to share,
The sequel of journeys, with flair and flair.
Like kaleidoscope colors swirl in the air,
We stitch together dreams with love and care.

So here's to the paths that twist and bend,
Where the map leads us, the fun won't end.
With each unexpected, a chuckle shines bright,
In the tapestry woven of chances and flight.

The Unveiling of Hidden Stories

Within the attic, secrets lie deep,
Tangled tales that make one leap.
A dusty box, what treasures unfold,
The remnants of laughter, amusing and bold.

An old love letter, with scribbles and stains,
Speaking of heroics and silly refrains.
Faded photographs, giggles in tow,
Zooming through memories, where did they go?

With each trinket, a riddle appears,
The past stretching wide, connecting our years.
Peeking through windows, the laughter resounds,
In every heartbeat, the joy still abounds.

So let's raise the veil, and uncover the cheer,
In shadows of stories, both far and near.
The joy of the past invited to play,
In the dance of the present, we'll sway and stay.

The Taste of an Unfinished Feast

A banquet spread with joyful mess,
Half-eaten cake and some old dress.
The ice cream melts, a puddle sighs,
As giggles float and mischief flies.

Leftovers dance upon the plate,
A hint of spice that tempts our fate.
The punch was spiked with jokes galore,
While Auntie tripped, we begged for more.

Forks are flung in playful fights,
Nibbles stolen on wild nights.
We laugh and snack, then take a break,
To plot a plan, to bake and wake.

When dessert is late, we shout with glee,
It's not just food, but revelry.
The taste of fun, forever near,
In every crumb, we share our cheer.

Where the Sun Meets Immediate Plans

With sunhats on, we plot our schemes,
To chase the light or chase our dreams.
An ice cream truck rolls down the street,
We chase it down with dancing feet.

A beach ball bounces, soaring high,
While seagulls steal the sandwiches nigh.
The waves will wait, but we won't tarry,
Our laughter's contagious, never wary.

Flip-flops fly, a game of tags,
Our worries dissolve as each joy drags.
An impromptu swim, the towels tossed,
In silly moments, we're never lost.

As the sun dips low, we raise a cheer,
For every plan we hold so dear.
Immediate bliss, a ray of fun,
Where every second's a golden run.

Whims of Irresolute Hearts

Two minds collide in quirky ways,
Should we dance or join a craze?
Pajamas worn as pants outside,
For whimsy's sake, we take a ride.

A donut shop at half past three,
We ponder flavors, wild and free.
A sprinkle war breaks the calm air,
With frosting smiles, we dance without care.

An endless list, we draw and scratch,
Chasing whims with every batch.
To sing out loud or stay discreet?
Our hearts are fickle, oh, such a treat.

Adventure waits, there's much to share,
In every giggle, we find a flare.
We paint the world with colors bright,
Through winding paths, we seek delight.

Moments That Linger Unseen

Sneaky whispers float in the air,
As silly secrets lead us there.
A sock puppet show, spontaneous art,
Each laugh ignites a hopeful spark.

The clock ticks slow, but we don't mind,
In every tick, some joy we find.
With crumbs of cake and tales to tell,
The clock is laughing too, so well.

Forgotten plans lie all around,
Yet magic grows where fun is found.
With every chuckle, the world's anew,
In unfinished chaos, friendships brew.

So here we sit, with hearts aglow,
In moments lost, our spirits grow.
We weave a tale of laughs and scenes,
With echoes of joy in the spaces between.

Moments Caught Between Heartbeats

In a world where hiccups reign,
We dance to tunes that drive us insane.
With laughter echoing in our chest,
We chase the joy that's never at rest.

A trip, a fall, a pie in the face,
Worn-out shoes can't keep up the pace.
Yet through the chaos, we find our groove,
In mishaps, our spirits always move.

Jokes linger like a misty fog,
As thoughts race fast in a sleepy bog.
What's planned may twist, ultimately bend,
We laugh and grumble, our best blend.

So here's a toast to clumsy surprise,
To bursting bubbles and gummy pies.
In each heartbeat, there's just one thing—
Let humor guide, it's the best fling.

The Art of Starting Over

With a wink to yesterday's grand scheme,
We toss our plans in the washing machine.
Out comes a shirt, two sizes too small,
But hey, it's gift-wrapped, let's share it all!

We scribble notes on wobbly chairs,
With every flop, we're muting our cares.
Restarting feels like a comical dance,
With two left feet, we still take a chance.

A soggy sandwich becomes a feast,
Mismatched socks, the fashion beast.
In shambles and giggles, we find our spine,
In the art of do-overs, we intertwine.

So here's to fresh starts with a silly grin,
With each misstep, we begin again.
Crafting memories like a whimsical pot,
In the flurry of failure, we'll find our spot.

Revelry in the Face of Delay

The clock ticks slower than a turtle's race,
As we sip our drinks with a chuckle in place.
With unforeseen pauses, we craft a jest,
Wasting time has never felt so blessed.

Quirky stories spill like popcorn in flight,
Chasing the hours with all of our might.
Each chuckle echoes in the waiting room,
As we conjure up fog in the light of gloom.

Events left hanging—a curious thrill,
With plans that teeter and dare to spill.
Yet we embrace the messy, the wild at heart,
Delaying our worries, we paint our art.

So here's to waiting—let's raise a cheer,
In maze of time, let's disappear.
Finding joy in the bumps in the road,
Our playful spirit will lighten the load.

Sipping Memories Under a Starlit Sky

Under a quilt of twinkling dreams,
We garden our thoughts like wildflower beams.
In mugs of warmth, we brew we time,
As laughter flows like a bubbling rhyme.

We gather stories like colorful beads,
From mishaps to dreams, in humorous feeds.
Each pop and fizz becomes a delight,
In the twilight, worry takes flight.

Unseen paths twist like a toddler's dance,
Every hiccup is just circumstance.
Under the stars, with hearts open wide,
The glow of smiles becomes our guide.

So here's to moments, both raucous and sweet,
With a splash of delight in every heartbeat.
In the charm of the night, we'll sip and share,
Creating magic with alchemy rare.

Whispers at Dawn

In morning's glow, we trip and tumble,
With sleepy grins, our voices rumble.
The coffee brews like bubbling joy,
As toast pops up, a golden toy.

We dance with socks that don't quite match,
The cat looks on, a silent watch.
A cereal spill, oh what a sight,
We laugh out loud, hearts feeling light.

A sock survives but meets its end,
As mismatched mates refuse to blend.
With every laugh, a memory grows,
In mornings bright, that's how it goes.

So here we stand, with all our quirks,
A polka dot chase that never jerks.
Just silly smiles, we take the chance,
As dawn unfurls, we start to dance.

The Dance of Half-Closed Doors

A door ajar, with much to say,
It creaks and squeaks, in a funny way.
Pat sliding in, then out, quick quiz,
Turning like a pro, it's all a fizz.

Half-hearted steps, a clumsy glide,
With giggles trapped, we can't abide.
The hallway's echo shows our flair,
As secret whispers fill the air.

A peek around, a shoe misplaced,
In games of hide, we laugh and chase.
With every twist, a story spun,
In half-closed doors, we find the fun.

So let the laughter spill and soar,
As we tumble into every door.
For joy is found in silly tours,
In all our steps, the heart assures.

Jests in the Gentle Breeze

A breeze so soft, it tells a tale,
Of careless pranks, a feathered sail.
With hats askew, we chase the wind,
While nature giggles, our hearts rescind.

A picnic basket tips and rolls,
Bananas fly like tiny goals.
We dodge and weave, with laughter bold,
As stories from our youth unfold.

The shadows dance beneath the trees,
As we attempt our silliest tease.
With every chuckle, we break the norm,
In gentle breezes, we find the warm.

So here's to fun, in every breeze,
To countless jests, we'll never freeze.
As laughter spills like summer rain,
In gentle winds, our joy's unchained.

When Dreams Take a Pause

Nestled tight, the world fades grey,
As dreams decide to take a sway.
With cotton clouds where giggles float,
We sail on waves of a sleepy boat.

Yet from the dusk, a voice does peep,
"Why not join in? It's time to leap!"
With tangled sheets, we try to roll,
And find the humor in every goal.

Caught mid-yawn, we snort and chuckle,
With morning breath, we can't help but buckle.
The dreamland calls with silly grace,
In every pause, we find our place.

So when the night holds dreams in sway,
We'll laugh and jest, come what may.
With light-hearted hearts, we take the chance,
When dreams subside, we still can dance.

The Light of Distant Stars

Twinkling tales from faraway spheres,
Echoes of laughter, it's music to ears.
We chase the dreams that zoom through the night,
With wishes that twinkle, oh what a sight!

Fumbling our way with shoes on the wrong feet,
Balancing ice cream on a fast-moving seat.
Stars spill their secrets, we giggle and sway,
As giggles become stars, lighting our way!

Curious comets with quirky designs,
Leave trails of chuckles, and playful signs.
Asteroids waltz, making mischief anew,
As we join the dance, just us and a few!

Distant stars beckon with bright, silly charms,
Collecting our chaos in cosmic farms.
So here's to the journey, let joy take the lead,
In the mess we're crafting, let's plant every seed!

Shades of Unfinished Portraits

A canvas adorned with splashes that shout,
Colors collide as giggles flit about.
Brush strokes are bold, but the edges are blurred,
In this gallery of chaos, no judgment is heard.

Pieces of laughter painted with flair,
Smudges of joy spread everywhere.
The palette is vibrant, yet oddly askew,
As we dip our brushes in colors so true.

Each portrait tells stories, both jumbled and bright,
Unfinished, yet perfect in its garish delight.
With a wink and a nudge, we laugh as we see,
The art of existence is wild and carefree!

So here's to the whims, the mix-ups, the fun,
Canvas of giggles, it's only begun.
In shades of our stories, we paint side by side,
Creating a masterpiece we'll never hide!

The Journey So Far

With snacks in our bags and a quirky old map,
We've traveled through giggles, and sometimes a clap.
Steps full of stumbles, we've danced in the rain,
Swapping tales with trees, forgetful but sane.

Lost in the wild, we followed our hearts,
Making new friends with each twist and start.
From picnic mishaps to laughter on trails,
Our moments are tales that swell like big sails!

With each twist of fate, we chuckle and grin,
Collecting our stories like treasures within.
So here's to the paths that led us astray,
In the mess of our travels, we find our own way!

A journey of whimsy, with joy as our guide,
Turning each stumble into a wild ride.
So pack up your laughter and join in the spree,
For the journey keeps rolling, as happy as can be!

Scribbles on a Forgotten Notebook

A notebook lay hidden, its corners all frayed,
Filled with wild nonsense and thoughts that we laid.
Catchy doodles of dreams and a prank or two,
In scribbles of laughter, our madness shines through.

Lost in the margins, bizarre little lines,
Jokes written awkwardly, quirky designs.
Each page a party, a moment in time,
Where giggles spill freely, and nonsense can rhyme.

From half-baked ideas to plans that went wrong,
This treasure of chaos deserves its own song.
With wobbly letters, we dance as we write,
Creating our symphony of silly delight.

So here's to the scribbles, the laughter we share,
In forgotten notebooks, we find our wild flair.
With joy in our hearts and a quill in our hands,
Let's craft a new story where chuckles expand!

Shadows of Forgotten Smiles

In corners where the giggles hide,
Shadows dance with memories tied.
A banana peel on the old stone wall,
Reminds us how we took a fall.

Jokes left hanging, like clothes on a line,
Twisted humor, oh how divine!
The cat takes a leap, then steers clear,
As we laugh at all the silly fear.

Tickling the funny bone, so sly,
While we chase clouds drifting by.
Old stories brewing in a teacup,
Echo faintly, "Hey, look up!"

In the cracks where laughter spills wide,
We find joy that was cast aside.
So we dance with the echoes and grin,
For in each jest, new tales begin.

The Melodies of What Could Be

Notes that linger on the breeze,
Harmony in whispers and tease.
A broken string on a guitar,
Plays the tune of a near star.

Chasing stars with bottles in hand,
We dream of places quite unplanned.
The ice cream truck, a resounding chime,
Takes us back, stretching time.

Imaginary hats upon our heads,
Each one stitched with words unsaid.
In the crowd, we're the merry few,
Turning frowns to dancing rue.

With every giggle we rewrite fate,
Building castles while we wait.
In the silence where colors collide,
We sit back and enjoy the ride.

Raindrops on Worn Pathways

Puddles laugh as we jump in,
Splashing hopes where the murk begins.
A forgotten umbrella, quite a show,
As the sky plays a game of throw.

Worn out shoes tell tales of fun,
Chasing moments till the day is done.
Raindrops dance, a whimsical beat,
Immediate joy beneath our feet.

Frogs sing loudly from mint green reeds,
Nonsense blooms from genuine needs.
With umbrellas turned inside out,
We skip ahead, heart full of doubt.

Under grey skies, we paint a smile,
Making every step worth the while.
Let the heavens open, let it pour,
As we laugh, asking for more.

Chasing the Light in Dusk

Fading colors swirl and mix,
With laughter, we're ready for our kicks.
Chasing fireflies, we spin around,
In this twilight, joy is found.

Whispers rising with the night,
As the moon peeks with delight.
We trip on shadows and giggle loud,
In this playful, bustling crowd.

Dust bunnies dance, nobody cares,
Exciting tales float in the air.
With every laugh, an echo bends,
Writing stories with imaginary pens.

And when the last light starts to creep,
We forge ahead, no time for sleep.
What lies ahead, we can't quite see,
But the chase is where we long to be.

The Stillness Between the Punchlines

In the quiet of the jest, we pause,
A hiccup in the chatter, a joke with flaws.
The punchlines dance just out of reach,
Tickling the ribs as they quietly breach.

Whispers of wit float through the air,
Giggling shadows, beyond compare.
Each giggle holds a secret smile,
Witty comebacks, waiting a while.

The stillness begs for laughter to bloom,
In the anticlimax, the jokes find room.
A tickle in the chest, a gleam in the eye,
Waiting for the moment when the punchlines fly.

So here we linger, in chuckles we stay,
With every muffled giggle, we find our way.
The stop before the humor takes flight,
In the stillness of punchlines, all feels right.

Chronicles of Smiles Yet to Be Written

Pages of joy still waiting to turn,
Where every corner has tales to learn.
A wink from fortune, a twist of fate,
In the chronicles of chuckles, we celebrate.

Ink runs dry on the jokes unsaid,
We tiptoe through moments, laughter widespread.
Each grin a chapter, each chuckle a word,
In stories of giggles, absurdity stirred.

So grab your pens and join the spree,
In the saga of smiles, come laugh with me.
We'll sketch out moments, both merry and grand,
In the margins of mirth, let good times expand.

Unwritten laughter awaits our delight,
As we scribble through days, from morn until night.
With grand pens of humor, let's fill every page,
In the chronicles of joy, we'll laugh through each stage.

The Bridge Between What Was and What Could Be

Balancing on beams of anecdotes shared,
A wire of memories, carefully bared.
With each step, a flicker of glee,
As we straddle the past and what's yet to be.

The echoes giggle as they glide along,
Past moments flirt, to a humorous song.
In this wobbly dance, we tango with fate,
Building bridges with punchlines, we celebrate.

The joke from yesterday, a wiggle today,
As we bounce between whimsy and sway.
A leap into laughter, from pain and regret,
On this bridge, there's a new life to be met.

So sway with the rhythm, embrace the unknown,
Turn the quirks of the past to a chuckle, your own.
For beyond this crossing, joy isn't far,
Together we'll wander, to where the smiles are.

Shadows of Tomorrow's Laughter

Beneath the glow of a gigglelight moon,
Shadows of chuckles begin to swoon.
Each whisper a secret, each grin a tale,
In the fading daylight, where puns prevail.

Tomorrow's humor dances on the brink,
It tickles the air, as we pause to think.
Will we fashion tomorrow with smiles so bright?
In shadows we ponder, in laughter's light.

With every snicker, a glimpse of the day,
In the shadows of future, we'll find our way.
Behind every joke, a tomorrow that gleams,
With echoes of laughter, igniting our dreams.

So let's craft a path, where giggles abound,
In the laughter of tomorrows, we'll surely be found.
With joy in our pockets and quirks on the side,
We'll chase down the shadows where humor does hide.

www.ingramcontent.com/pod-product-compliance
Lightning Source LLC
Chambersburg PA
CBHW051638160426
43209CB00004B/695